P9-DGC-386

RELEASE GOD'S WORD
TO EVERY LIFE SITUATION
AND WATCH IT WORK

EXPERIENCING
THE POWER
OF GOD'S WORD

Dr. Clarice Fluitt

Foreword by Sid Roth

Experiencing the Power of God's Word © 2017 Clarice Fluitt

All rights reserved. This book is protected by the copyright laws of the United States of America. This book may not be reproduced in any form, stored in a retrieval system, or transmitted in any form by any means; electronic, mechanical, photocopy, recording, scanning, or otherwise; without prior written permission of the author except as provided by United States of America copyright law. Unless otherwise noted, Scripture quotations are from the King James Version of the Bible (Public Domain). In some instances, they are author's paraphrases. Scripture quotations marked (AMP) taken from the Amplified® Bible, Copyright © 2015 by The Lockman Foundation. Used by permission. (www.Lockman.org) Scripture quotations marked (AMPC) taken from the Amplified® Bible, Classic Edition Copyright © 1954, 1958, 1962, 1964, 1965, 1987 by The Lockman Foundation. Used by permission. (www.Lockman.org) Scripture quotation marked (NIV) taken from the New International Version®. Copyright © 1973, 1978, 1984, 2011 by Biblica, Inc. Used by permission. Scripture quotation marked (NKJV) taken from the New King James Version®. Copyright © 1982 by Thomas Nelson, Inc. Used by permission. All rights reserved.

Publisher: Clarice Fluitt Enterprises, LLC

P O Box 15111 Monroe, LA 71207

claricefluitt.com

ISBN: 978-0-9903694-8-6

EXPERIENCING
THE POWER
OF GOD'S WORD

Acknowledgments

What it is like to live inside the power of God's Word is the epitome of the lives of my co-laborers in this project; Dr. Tandie Mazule, Dr. Evon Peet, and Carol Martinez. The separate and distinct contributions each has made to this literary endeavor bridges the gap between standing alone, and making a whole. Their dedication to perfection is unmatched, their commitment to the vision of another is only realized as they make it their own, and their sense of accomplishment toward a standard of excellence marks the accomplishment of this finished project.

Ask any of them what effect God's Word has had on their lives and each could give a brilliant accounting of having lived a life positioned as witnesses to His unmatchable grace, deepest mysteries, and most profound victories. All three are living examples of having experienced the power of God's Word, released it into their own lives, and watched it work in ways that are above and beyond what anyone could possibly think or imagine!

Endorsements

Occasionally in this life you will meet someone who resonates with such similar opinions as your own that you immediately sense you have known that person forever. Their personality, intellect, and passion for life so absorbs and reflects your own that what they write and speak causes your heart to leap and cry, "That's it! That's the glory! That's the Spirit of the Lord." Dr. Clarice Fluitt has that kind of impact on my wife Bonnie and me. Her new book, *Experiencing the Power of God's Word* does that.

Through her accurate and time-proven prophetic voice in *Experiencing the Power of God's Word*, Dr. Clarice Fluitt raises a clarion call to release the Word over every life-challenging situation. Funny, wise, and passionately in love with Jesus, Dr. Clarice draws from her rich reservoir of a lifelong testimony of proving God's faithfulness to His word when we speak it. In these pages, she skillfully shares that experience and knowledge to provide you with strategies that will guide you to an encounter with God's spoken word.

Your day to see the Word make a way where there is no way, lay hold of your turn around, command your breakthrough, and cause you to rise from your present state of strength, faith, and provision, to that place where Jesus is speaking His better things for you and your family, is here.

Experiencing the Power of God's Word carries the impartation you want and need. Get it. Read it. Act on it. And see results through The Power of God's Word!

MAHESH AND BONNIE CHAVDA
CHAVDA MINISTRIES INTERNATIONAL &
THE WATCH OF THE LORD
ALL NATIONS CHURCH, CHARLOTTE, NORTH CAROLINA

I had the pleasure of getting to know Dr. Clarice Fluitt several years ago, and I loved her from the first word she spoke.

Her stories, Bible teachings, and life message all resonated within not only my heart but every single person in the room where she spoke. In her new book, *Experiencing the Power of God's Word*, Dr. Fluitt shares all the stories wrapped within the Word of God that made her who she is today.

You will laugh; you will cry; you will see glimpses of yourself in the pages of this book. And, oh, what a miraculous journey God has taken Dr. Fluitt on. *Experiencing the Power of God's Word* will encourage and awaken your heart again to see the hand of God at the very core and framework of your life. You simply will not be able to put it down.

JULIE MEYER

SANTA MARIA APOSTOLIC CENTER

Table of Contents

Foreword

*G*rab hold of your faith, see for yourself, and experience the excitement of living in the realm of miracles. This book will teach you key nuggets that will empower you to believe God for the impossible. So, welcome to my world, where it's naturally supernatural, and no longer be a spectator but step into your destiny.

Dr. Clarice captures the essence of the entire book in one such powerful story of the journey she took watching her 13-year-old daughter go from innocence to drug addiction in the blink of an eye then, 27 years later, seeing the victory in her daughter's life, and the answer to her prayers manifested. From the outset, Dr. Clarice had only one option; to declare God's Word over the debilitating and excruciating toll that drugs took in the life of her daughter, and believe that His Word had more power than this addiction. She chose to never give up, and never lost heart or faith that what God's Word said was a higher truth than the reality she saw with her natural eyes. As you read the full accounting of this marvelous and miraculous story, I pray that her testimony from personal tragedy to profound victory will encourage you to choose to daily agree with God's Word and decree it in the face of all adversities which try to confuse you from embracing the truth.

In the simplest and most practical of ways, Dr. Fluitt shows you how the powerful effects of God's Word released over every situation can change every negative existing state of affairs in your life to be reversed and actually become upgrades and your strengths.

Every once in a while, a book comes along that strikes at the very core of change. It influences decisions, remakes the multitudes, repurposes the prospects, and redefines the destinations. We all need a starting point. Because you desire to add another dimension to your ever-evolving life of change; because you want to experience God's power and provision in your life; because you desire a transformed life; should you need a starting point or a jumping off point, *Experiencing the Power of God's Word* is your answer to the beginning, the end, and everything in between.

Dr. Clarice Fluitt has spent over four decades establishing herself and gathering simple but practical ways that show you how the powerful effects of God's Word released over every situation in your life can change every negative existing state of affairs into a positive and exciting undertaking. Hundreds of thousands have already been touched by Dr. Clarice Fluitt. She has appeared on my "It's Supernatural!" program and I know for a fact you will find yourself eager to apply the practical instructions contained in this book to your own personal situations.

This book is a composite of wisdom that is the natural outgrowth of personal experiential adventures and practical observations. It is marked by the kind of impartation that you can immediately apply to your life, addresses situations and circumstances that belong to all of us and, the best part of all, the advice contained and condensed in these pages works!

SID ROTH

HOST, "IT'S SUPERNATURAL!"

The Sovereign Turn of Events

But God has chosen the foolish things of the world to put to shame the wise, and God has chosen the weak things of the world to put to shame the things which are mighty. – 1 Corinthians 1:27

Chapter 1

*L*earning to see with the eyes of your heart is an amazing gift of the Holy Spirit. My mother had this awesome ability. Let me introduce you to Mama.

She was orphaned when she was five years old. Her mother died shortly after giving birth to her fifth child, so Mama and all of her siblings were separated from their father and other family and placed in a Baptist orphanage.

Now, before you get too sad, let me tell you what I know – *champions live differently than other people.*

Mama was introduced to Jesus while in the orphanage. She would often tell me the stories of her challenging childhood but always concluded with the positive, faith building words of encouragement, "The devil meant evil but God meant good." I would feel so proud as she spoke of how she became an honor student; a true overcomer who never saw herself as limited in any way.

Mama was Baptist in every way! We lived two doors down from Temple Baptist Church and were a seven-day-a-week church-going family.

Mama was a great Sunday School teacher. She was very smart, very beautiful, very strong, and very Baptist. She did not believe that a woman could or should teach a man, or even teach where a man might be. Women had no place of authority in the church except to teach other women, sing in the choir, cook, clean, take care of kids, and be silent. I did not inherit her strict point of view but I did truly love the Lord.

When I grew up, I did the unimaginable; I married a man that was more Catholic than the Pope. Mama was devastated! We had a time of religious confusion, but God quickly cleared the murky waters. While Mama was praying in her backyard, she had an amazing vision from the eyes of her heart. She saw me standing before great crowds of people preaching the Gospel. Then, she saw my husband also preaching. She was transformed by seeing into the unseen realm of God. All her opinions concerning "women preachers" were gone! She began to agree with the vision and speak the Word of God over the creative will of God.

When Mama told me and my husband, George, that she knew it was the will of God for him and me to become preachers, we both snickered and I said, "Mama, you sat too long in the sun." She smiled and said, "You're right. I have been sitting in the presence of the Lord and you two are called to preach." George and I were the most unlikely candidates to be called to preach. George's desire was to be a millionaire, and mine was to spend his money.

I would visit Mama and refuse to even enter her house until she turned off the Gospel music she was always listening to. If that wasn't bad enough, once I did enter the house, she would call me her little preacher girl. I reacted in a way that, I'm sure, was not very Christ-like. The very idea; I was as mad as a wet hen as she continued to activate the Word of God flowing from her mouth! I had no faith or desire to believe what Mama was saying, or especially that preacher name she called me.

But God has chosen the foolish things of the world to put to shame the wise, and God has chosen the weak things of the world to put to shame the things which are mighty. – 1 Corinthians 1:27 (NKJV)

In the midst of all my unbelief, I began to recall my childhood experience when I was in the third grade and very impressionable. I vividly remember hearing my Sunday School teacher say, "The Lord told me to trust Him with my life." I had never heard the Lord speak. Questions filled my mind. How did she **hear** the voice of God? What did it sound like?

I dearly loved my Sunday School teacher. She was the typical southern grandmother: beautiful white hair, a bit rotund, with twinkling Santa Claus eyes, and a kind and encouraging word for everyone. I would say to myself, "When I grow up, I want to be just like her!"

I asked her how she heard God's voice. She smiled and said,

"Oh, Honey, I don't hear Him with my natural ears," then she quoted the Scripture from John 8:28, *I only say what I hear the father say.* "I hear Him with the ears in my H-ear-t," she said. I did not know that we had ears in our heart. I was young with much to learn. My teacher was patient with my youth and lack of understanding and explained the meaning of this verse. This became a life-changing Scripture for me.

As I grew in my own faith, the understanding that my spiritual eyes and ears reside in my spiritual heart ultimately became a reality. After searching the Scriptures, I became enlightened by the Holy Spirit, and when God's Word said that I could hear God and see visions, I chose to agree with Him. By faith, I positioned myself to learn how to recognize the voice of God and train my spiritual ears to hear the inaudible, and my spiritual eyes to see the unseen.

> *By faith, I positioned myself to learn how to recognize the voice of God and train my spiritual ears to hear the inaudible, and my spiritual eyes to see the unseen.*

While I was still wrestling with Mama's decrees to be her little preacher girl, I visited a friend and found myself telling her that I wanted to know more about God. She said, "Just tell Him you want to know Him." All it took was for me to say, "If there really is a God, reveal Yourself to me." And then I said, "I want to trust You with my life."

For My thoughts are not your thoughts, Nor are your ways My ways," says the Lord. For as the heavens are higher than

the earth, So are My ways higher than your ways, And My
thoughts than your thoughts. – Isaiah 55:8-9 (NKJV)

At this time, I was not cognizant that the prayer of my heart was exactly what my third grade Sunday School teacher had spoken long ago. It had quickened my interest in hearing the voice of God and had come full circle. Two days later, I sovereignly received the baptism of the Holy Spirit, and Mama had her preacher girl. The amazing truth that God's Word accomplishes what it is sent to accomplish had become an undeniable truth in my life. Thank God for Mama's steadfast faith and boldness to speak the Word of God from her heart when the facts said no, but grace said yes.

Mama's faith was to fuel the manifestation of God's will with the spoken Word of God that served to activate the will of God. The creative will of God was that I was called to preach, and I have done exactly that for over 40 years. Mama is in heaven now but she lived to see her vision and decrees manifested in her lifetime. She often said, because of my extreme passion and boldness, "Surely, I have over-prayed!"

Then the Lord said to me, "You have seen well, for I am ready
to perform My word." – Jeremiah 1:12 (NKJV)

Now let me share with you a sovereign turn of events about my Sunday School teacher. Her name was Mrs. Fluitt. She was a distant relative of my future husband's family. In the fullness of time, I became Mrs. Fluitt when I married my husband, George Marbury Fluitt. Remember, when I was in the third grade I said I wanted to be just like Mrs. Fluitt when I grew up. Your words are powerful. Be careful what you ask for! After becoming an ordained minister and pastoring a church, I received a letter from her. She told me she had prayed for me every day from the time I was in her class as a third-grade student. By then, she was 88 years old. The fuel of Mrs. Fluitt's faith helped to empower my life.

At this time, I have been on this amazing faith journey for over five decades and His voice is growing clearer each day. The beautiful Holy Spirit is my teacher and revelator that opened the eyes of my heart to see Jesus.

Here are some Scriptures that have helped me to understand that it is the will of God for His sheep (people) to know His voice and see visions:

He who has ears to hear, let him hear! – Matthew 11:15 (NKJV)

And He said to them, He who has ears to hear, let him hear! – Mark 4:9 (NKJV)

Also I heard the voice of the Lord, saying: "Whom shall I send, And who will go for Us?" Then I said, "Here am I! Send me." And He said, "Go, and tell this people: 'Keep on hearing, but do not understand; Keep on seeing, but do not perceive.' "Make the heart of this people dull, And their ears heavy, And shut their eyes; Lest they see with their eyes, And hear with their ears, And understand with their heart, And return and be healed." – Isaiah 6:8-10 (NKJV)

And when he brings out his own sheep, he goes before them; and the sheep follow him, for they know his voice. – John 10:4 (NKJV)

So he said, "I heard Your voice in the garden, and I was afraid because I was naked; and I hid myself." – Genesis 3:10 (NKJV)

In the following pages, I invite you to join me as we investigate the winding path to seeing the invisible and hearing the inaudible with the eyes and ears of faith that are located within your circumcised heart.

Notes

Cast Your Cares Upon the Lord....

Cast your cares on the Lord and He will sustain you; He will never let the righteous be shaken. – Psalm 55:22

Chapter 2

It is our biblical responsibility and privilege as Christians to both agree with God's Word and activate His will by decreeing and releasing His Word to every life situation.

While I continue to wear my heart on my sleeve, let me share another one of the many victorious testimonies I have experienced as I have learned to embrace the discipline that is essential for releasing God's Word as the antidote against principalities, powers, and rulers of the darkness of this world.

To many of us, the dearest and most important things in our lives are our family members. When any of our family suffer, we vicariously feel their pain and our faith can be shaken if we look at the problem rather than the solution. This is how I learned to release the power of God's Word over my own personal family tragedy. I had to choose to speak the positive truth (God's Word) over my very painful evidence that was, at one time, the reality of my daughter's life.

My daughter came to me crying telling me she had been given a marijuana cigarette. She was only 13 years old. Most unfortunately, this one rebellious act opened a satanic door to a heart-breaking lifestyle that led to her multiple prison sentences from one end of the country to the other, and a long journey into the darkest of life choices.

> *When circumstances would look the worst and the long raging battle for her life seemed unbeatable, I continued to strengthen myself with God's promise.*

When circumstances would look the worst and the long raging battle for her life seemed unbeatable, I continued to strengthen myself with God's promise: All of my children are disciples taught of the Lord and great is their peace and undisturbed composure.

And all your [spiritual] children shall be disciples [taught by the Lord and obedient to His will], and great shall be the peace and undisturbed composure of your children.
– Isaiah 54:13 (AMPC)

This story should be a movie because so many people have a similar sad story of how drugs, alcohol, and wrong relationships have been their painful and frustrating experience.

In the face of ever-increasing negative and discouraging reports, year after year I continued to agree with and speak God's Word to activate His creative will for my daughter:

Before I formed you in the womb I knew you; Before you were born I sanctified you; I ordained you a prophet to the nations. – Jeremiah 1:5 (NKJV)

One year, only two days before Mother's Day, my daughter called to tell me that within three days she was due to appear before a Commissioner in Daytona, Florida, for an arraignment to schedule a hearing.

On very short notice, I made arrangements to travel from Louisiana to Florida. On the day of her arraignment, I eventually found the location and got seated. Approximately 45 prisoners were brought into the room to be assigned to their new locations. They were all handcuffed and shackled, had orange prison suits on, and were called by numbers, not their names. The impact of the spirit of grief flowing from the visiting loved ones in that hot crowded room was heart breaking. When the bailiff called their number, they went before the commissioner, their charge was identified and then they were immediately taken out of the room to be loaded onto their respective transport buses. I was seated in the back of the room. When my daughter entered the room, her number was called, which I quickly wrote down, and without a thought I involuntarily came to my feet and said, "Sir, prisoner number . . . . is mine. Sir, Sunday is Mother's Day. I cannot see how it would serve the great state of Florida to house and feed this prisoner. Sir, I am her mother and I ask you to release her into my custody. I'm here to take her home."

The Commissioner was obviously dazed and amazed at my audacity. His first comments were that he was not the Judge and had no jurisdiction or authority to release her. On the heels of this comment, he turned to the bailiff and said, "Cut her loose." My daughter was shocked, the whole room went silent, and miracle of miracles, my daughter was released into my custody. I thought to myself, "Proverbs 28:1, ' . . .the righteous are as bold as a lion.' This is the miracle I have been waiting for. Everything will change now. All my prayers were surely being answered.'" The days of not knowing if she was dead or alive were over, I rejoiced. Now, all our lives would become normal. Great restoration would bless our home again. Thank You, Jesus!

It was such a joy to have my daughter back at home. She was as sweet as she could be. We were singing together, and weeping together for her freedom. This was like a precious dream that had come true. But to my great consternation, three days later she stole my clothes, flagged a truck, and took off to California with my credit card and anything else she could get in her bag. I took a deep breath and remembered that there is usually an Ishmael before there is an Isaac.

Would you still trust God if your life took this turn of events?

I suddenly experienced the overwhelming peace of God and I had no power to be angry. In my heart, I heard this Scripture, *And the peace of God, which surpasses all understanding, will guard your hearts and minds through Christ Jesus* (Philippians 4:7 NKJV). At that point, her love was drugs, and her senses had been dulled beyond reason. I felt the pain of it, but realized that at this time, she was not ready for any other lifestyle. This situation was not about her rebellion or her terrible choices. Her addiction to drugs had replaced any need for mother, father, brother, sister, and children, and had become her total and complete source of life. For the first time in this journey, I realized this was not about me and my pain; it was about hers.

After this incident, I remained in communication with her, although I only heard from her when she needed money. With each phone call, I reminded her of God's calling on her life, and continued to believe God for her deliverance.

She was again arrested, this time for stealing a pound of butter. This episode opened yet another can of worms, and her past once again tracked her down. At this point, the Lord told me to stop asking Him to do what He had already done. Her life was in His hands and I needed to start thanking Him and praising Him for His finished work.

For I know the thoughts that I think toward you, saith the Lord, thoughts of peace, and not of evil, to give you an expected end. –Jeremiah 29:11 (KJV)

She returned to her life of crime and overdosed on heroin. As fast as she slid into jail, she slid out. The person who was doing drugs with her left her to die, and it is believed this person called the police to let them know where my daughter was.

Cast your cares on the Lord and he will sustain you; he will never let the righteous be shaken. – Psalm 55:22 (NIV)

I received a heart-breaking call that my daughter had been found unconscious after taking an overdose of drugs. Upon her arrival at the hospital, she was put on 72 hours of life support, was diagnosed with no brain activity, and had a prognosis of significant brain damage with grim chances of any recovery. Even with this prognosis and little, if any, chance of recovery, recover she did! Not only did brain and life activity resume, she found herself leaving the hospital – but only to be immediately returned to jail.

She was once again scheduled to go before a Judge for sentencing. I had become acquainted with one of my daughter's counselors who had a tremendous gift of faith toward my daughter, and who accompanied her to the sentencing. The Judge's words to my daughter were, "After reviewing your case, you have to be one of the most despicable, incorrigible plights on society. Do you have anything to say before I sentence you?" This was my daughter's reply, "Sir, half of what I've done, you don't even know about; but, this I know, I come from a line of champions and I have been created for greatness. My actions do not determine who I actually am." The Judge carefully considered his response. Miraculously, she was given an eight-year joint suspension but told that if there was even the slightest infraction, she would go to jail to serve her entire eight-year sentence.

When challenges come your way, remember, 1 Corinthians 16:13: *Be on your guard; stand firm in the faith; be courageous; be strong.*

She entered the recovery program and, like the prodigal son, came to her senses, repented, completed her sentence, successfully graduated from the drug court program, and found her purpose. The same Judge that had sentenced her earlier was at her graduation and said of my daughter with tears in his eyes, "This woman's story is much like the story of Lazarus being raised from the dead. Truly, she is a new woman."

Let us not become weary in doing good, for at the proper time we will reap a harvest if we do not give up. – Galatians 6:9 (NIV)

My precious daughter was restored to our family, her children, her health, and her gifts and talents and now lives an abundant life physically, spiritually, and financially. She went back to college and studied drug and alcohol counseling with a major in psychology, graduated, and interned with a doctor who is an industry leader in comprehensive wellness and recovery care. She is now the Executive Director of the only luxury residential treatment facility on the central coast of California. She daily contributes to serving the challenged community that she has been delivered from.

This was my daughter's reply, "Sir, half of what I've done, you don't even know about; but, this I know, I come from a line of champions and I have been created for greatness. My actions do not determine who I actually am."

Jesus looked at them and said, "With man this is impossible, but not with God; all things are possible with God. – Mark 10:27 (NIV)

This journey took 27 long years!

Have I not commanded you? Be strong and courageous. Do not be afraid; do not be discouraged, for the Lord your God will be with you wherever you go. – Joshua 1:9 (NIV)

I rejoice over God's faithfulness to watch over His Word to perform it, but I know that I also had a responsibility to decree His Word.

To Him who alone does great wonders, For His mercy endures forever. –Psalm 136:4 (NKJV)

I pray that this testimony will encourage you to choose to daily agree with God's Word and decree it in the face of all adversities which try to confuse you from embracing the truth.

I read the end of God's Book, and we have already won.

Seeing Things from God's Perspective

Yet for us there is but one God, the Father, from whom all things came and for whom we live; and there is but one Lord, Jesus Christ, through whom all things came and through whom we live. –1 Corinthians 8:6 (NIV)

Chapter 3

The Scripture teaches that "The earth and the fullness of it belongs to God" (Psalm 24:1). As born-again believers, we are part of the fullness of God and are the only legitimate joint heirs with Christ. We have been given dominion in the earth and throughout eternity. God calls and equips us to have dominion. I think that is so incredible! The Lord says, "Now, I'm going to take everything I am and all that I have and share it with you." Part of us being in covenant with God is that anytime He gives us an assignment, He promises, "I have given you everything that you need to succeed." We always come totally and completely equipped with everything necessary to be victorious in life. We must choose to speak the Word of God.

I get so excited when I have little glimpses of the demonstrations and manifestations of the power of God. I believe that when we begin to investigate how to live in the supernatural realm, God will show us how to make time our servant. We are called and equipped to be a sign and a wonder. Jesus told us that as we go our way, we are to say, "The Kingdom of God has come in me. Heal the sick. Raise the dead. Cast out demons, and preach good news."

> *For us to prosper and be in health as our soul prospers, we must not only have faith in God, but rather have the faith of God.*

As we learn to embrace God's truth and choose to step outside of natural limitations into an eternal realm, we will hear God calling us to ascend and see things from His perspective. He is high above all principalities, powers, and problems. The devil is a totally defeated foe. The only thing that works is his lying mouth. Norman Vincent Peale wrote, "It seems there is an invisible reservoir of abundance in the universe that can be tapped into by obeying certain spiritual laws. God will pass over a million people just to find someone who believes Him. Faith will not necessarily prevent all mountains, but it will move them! The God kind of faith is an absolute necessity in this life." For us to prosper and be in health as our soul prospers, we must not only have faith in God, but rather have the faith of God.

> *I have been crucified with Christ; it is no longer I who live, but Christ lives in me; and the life which I now live in the flesh I live by faith in the Son of God, who loved me and gave Himself for me. – Galatians 2:20 (NKJV)*

I believe that there has been a divine shift happening in the earth's atmosphere! I have a friend whose name is Joshua Mills. Joshua is a young man that God uses to literally change the atmosphere and invade the realm of miracles. As he speaks the Word of God, incredible miracles take place. He has all kinds of manifestations of jewels falling as well as oil and gold coming out of his hands; he just keeps preaching right through it. Gold dust is all over his shoes, and then it begins to appear on the people that he is teaching! He wrote a book on how to change the atmosphere. Do you believe that you are called to change your atmosphere with the Word of God?

We were born again to create the atmosphere of heaven here on earth. God invites us to come by faith and be seated in heavenly places, see what He sees, speak like He speaks. Simply speaking, God responds to His own words in everything we say and do that gives Him glory.

Yet for us there is but one God, the Father, from whom all things came and for whom we live; and there is but one Lord, Jesus Christ, through whom all things came and through whom we live.
–1 Corinthians 8:6 (NIV)

All things were made through Him, and without Him nothing was made that was made. – John 1:3 (NKJV)

God has made all things from before the beginning of time. Just think about the word "made." Everything that God has ever made or prepared is equipped with everything that is needed or required to fulfill God's will for you.

Notes

The Kingdom of God Is Voice-Activated by Speaking God's Word

And whatever Adam called each living creature, that was its name. Selah!

– Genesis 2:19, NKJV

Chapter 4

*M*y prayer: "Father, thank You for this opportunity to proclaim Your Word. Thank You that, as we hear Your Word, we will not only be hearers but doers of Your Word. In Jesus mighty and wondrous name, we decree that all power in heaven and earth has been invested in us. We will not just be informed but transformed by the power of Your Word. Lord, Your Word has the power to perform itself. We are discovering our full potential in You. As we choose to order our conversation righteous, You will show the salvation of God. Jesus is the salvation of God and, when we see Him, we will be like Him. There is no other acceptable image in God's sight." Amen!

I am persuaded that there is a divine frequency which comes from eternity that is released when a believer faithfully proclaims the Word of God. The Kingdom of God is voice-activated by speaking God's Word. God did not hum us into existence, He spoke. In the principles of God, when you speak the Word of God, what works in one kingdom can also work in the negative kingdom. If the Kingdom of God is voice-activated, the kingdom of darkness can also be voice-activated with the words we speak.

In the midst of embracing the changes that the Lord brings in our life, most often the enemy will come against our mind and tell us that our position is not as important as someone else's position. Rather than recognizing and being pleased with what God has called you to be and being the best you can be at it, you take on a competitive mindset and say, "Well, I'm not a teacher, and I'm not this, and I'm not that." It is a challenge to enter into God's rest and be the best at what He has called you to be.

If we desire to be spiritual, we must learn to talk to the things that are waiting to appear in this natural realm. When we give a name to something, we actually have given it a nature. God said to Adam, "I'm going to bring all these creatures in front of you, and whatever you call them, that is what they are going to be. Whatever you call it, you will have given it a name and a nature."

Out of the ground the LORD *God formed every beast of the field and every bird of the air, and brought them to Adam to see what he would call them. And whatever Adam called each living creature, that was its name. Selah! – Genesis 2:19 (NKJV)*

How do we get all this invisible stuff that God said belongs to the believer? First, we have to agree with the Word of God before we can begin to perceive it. We see with our natural eyes but perceive the manifestations of glory with our spiritual eyes. When our natural ear hears glorious testimonies, our hope begins to rise like the tide because faith comes by hearing God's Word. Let us all start speaking life.

The spoken Word of God flowing from a true believer has the activating effect on the will of God. It is that which causes everything in the unseen realm to be manifested into the natural realm. We give names to everything. We might say, "I have the flu." Because we have given it a name, everything in hell can now say, "The believers say they have the flu." You will get what you say, whether negative or positive. When you begin to agree with the Word of God and call the things that are not as though they were, you are creating with God. Life and death are in the tongue. Remember, we are a people making choices.

> *The spoken Word of God flowing from a true believer causes everything in the unseen realm to be manifested into the natural realm.*

THIS IS SO POWERFUL!

43

Notes

It Was Over Before It Began

Eye has not seen, nor ear heard, nor have entered into the heart of man the things which God has prepared for those who love Him, but God has revealed them to us through His Spirit. – 1 Corinthians 2:9-10

Chapter 5

For we who have believed do enter that rest, as He has said:
"So I swore in My wrath, 'They shall not enter My rest,'
<u>although the works were finished from the foundation of the</u>
<u>world."</u> – Hebrews 4:3

We, however, live in limited understanding of eternal time and do not think from an eternal perspective. Before the foundation of the world, before anything was made, God said everything was finished. Everything that was ever needed, ever was, or ever will be, was finished from the foundation of all time. Do you agree with God's Word?

Before the foundation of the world, before time began, the works were finished. When you begin to understand what God is seeing, you will understand the Scripture that says God sits in the heavens and laughs His enemy into derision. This is so incredible.

The Word of God spoken by the believer activates God's will and brings that which has already been created into that which we can see or apprehend with our five senses.

Although He finished everything before it began, His ongoing purpose is being unveiled as we who are the believers are creating with Him by calling the things that are not to become the things that are. He finished it before He created time and space; in other words, everything was over before it began. If you want to think with the mind of God, then think from the end of the thing, not the beginning. Jesus was legally crucified from the foundation of the earth. Before anything was, the answer to everything was done, but it remains that all of this activity from God's finished work must be experienced in a time and space realm!

We tend to think that someday it is going to be this way, or this and that are going to happen, but the reality is, from God's perspective in the unseen realm, everything is finished.

As an example of the principle of the finished work, I would like to share a story. I was speaking at a business seminar in Los Angeles, CA. There was nothing different about this speaking commitment; it was my keynote message that I present in various forms and fashions at so many other speaking venues. This was strictly and purely a business seminar. I presented my message no differently than I always do, then packed up my belongings, and departed for home. A few months later I was in San Diego for yet another business seminar. As much as I love these venues and sharing my knowledge with others, I often find myself on the same tour but in a variety of different cities over a short period of time.

While in San Diego, I found myself backstage following a dance competition that is a normal part of the actual seminar for the audience members. I suddenly saw a young lady running up to me backstage and she excitedly asked if she could share her testimony with me. I was amazed to learn that she had been at the same seminar in Los Angeles where I had also spoken a few months before. She said that during my keynote message in Los Angeles, the Lord began to speak to her and showed her how different her life could be if she would give her heart to Him. The Spirit of God did a wondrous work in her following this revelation that she gladly received. She got saved and knew immediately that she could no longer live the life she had been living, or even live in the same area. She left her wicked ways behind, was totally and completely on fire for the Lord, and moved from Los Angeles to San Diego to be a part of a church in that city.

All of this was as a result of a message that I had no idea I was even delivering, to a lady I had never met, in a city that I was only traveling through, at a time that was the least expected. The message had not been delivered in a church, and had no aspect of traditional preaching; but, something in the words I spoke changed her life for good; forever. The power of the spoken word resulted in the manifestation of the finished work.

In the realm of the finished exists everything you ever desired or wanted, exceedingly, abundantly above what you could ask or even think. 1 Corinthians 2:9-10 says,

*Eye has not seen, nor ear heard, nor have entered into the heart of man the things which God has prepared for those who love Him, <u>but God has revealed **them** to us through His Spirit</u> ... .*

Yes, He has revealed them to your spirit, so your spirit begins to leap with joy every now and then as you agree with the Word of God. You begin to dare to believe for signs, wonders, and miracles. You dare to believe that people are going to jump out of wheelchairs, arms and legs are going to grow where they have never been before, blind eyes are going to be opened when you speak God's Word. You were created to be in charge with dominion and power to conduct the affairs of the Kingdom of God. It is time to believe that God has given you vitality and vigor regardless of your age. We have a better covenant than Sarah, Rahab, and all the other Old Testament saints.

You are going to see wholesale deliverance of people who have been bound by drugs, alcohol, and wrong relationships. They will come out of the midst of bondage on this earth and into a place of rest called "Jesus." The realm of the Spirit is the heritage of the saints!

Let me give you an example: Mary the mother of Jesus received a word from an angel that she would bring forth the Savior of the world. She asked a very interesting question, *How shall this be, seeing I know not a man?* (Luke 1:34 KJV). The angel replied, *Oh, with God, everything is possible,* because it was finished before it began. There is no natural explanation. Please try to eradicate your natural thinking out of your brain, because what I am going to say is not going to sound reasonable to you if you have to understand it with your natural mind. Please turn on the mind of Christ where all things are possible.

Mary hid these angelic words in her heart. You see, there are things God tells you that must stay hidden until you find the right person to tell them to. Here was Mary looking for somebody that had an experience like hers. She understood that her revelation was going to be costly. Every revelation brings a revolution and a new set of friends. She heard that Elizabeth, who had been barren and was too old to have a baby, was now pregnant, and the same angel that had appeared to her had also appeared to Elizabeth.

Mary visited Elizabeth. At the salutation of Mary to Elizabeth, Elizabeth's response was passionately and prophetically activated by the sound of Mary's voice. This is so amazing. Mary had to find somebody who was hearing the same faith frequency that she was hearing.

> *You were created to be in charge with dominion and power to conduct the affairs of the Kingdom of God. It is time to believe that God has given you vitality and vigor regardless of your age.*

Can you hear the invitation of the Father to come up and see what He sees, and be what He is?

Wonderful things happen when the divine goes looking for the prophetic that is going to agree with the finished work. That frequency, that voice of power and authority, has power to create with God. This is not reincarnation; it is incarnation. "It is no longer I, but Christ that lives." He hears your voice and knows you by name; knows how many hairs are on your head, and is involved with you emotionally and devotionally. You are His beloved child with an eternal and supernatural inheritance.

Every now and then somebody will come along who really understands that the Kingdom of God is voice-activated by the believer agreeing and speaking the Word of God.

When Mary went to see Elizabeth, all she said was, "Hello, Elizabeth." Elizabeth responded prophetically with a prophetic unction shout out. She said,

> But why is this granted to me, that the mother of my Lord should come to me? For indeed, as soon as the voice of your greeting sounded in my ears, the babe leaped in my womb for joy.

There are people who are carrying something that will connect with you if you just allow it to happen. Jesus was looking for John. That same spirit that raised Christ from the dead has quickened your mortal body. The Christ in you is looking for those clarion callers that will not be moved by what they see but will be moved by the Word of God. When Jonathan, the son of King Saul, heard David speak, at the sound of his voice, he loved him more than his own soul.

You have your own voice print and have been made to fit into harmony with God. Nobody has your sound or your voice print.

God hears it above everything else when you are agreeing with His Word. Your voice print may sound like a distant noise to the natural ear, but to God it is the sound of divine agreement.

Notes

The Believer's Rest

The Lord is calling you to exercise dominion. It does not have anything to do with gender, color, education, or status. You now have a new nature; you just look like a human.

Chapter 6

For indeed the gospel was preached to us as well as to them;
but the word which they heard did not profit them, not being
mixed with faith in those who heard it. –Hebrews 4:2

The Scripture reference describes those who, upon hearing the Word but not mixing it with faith, received no benefit. There is a big difference between simply hearing something and mixing it with faith. Those who take the Word of God and mix it with faith will go right into the realm of the unseen. They will begin to bring healing, deliverance, prosperity, joy, and peace because they know the earth and the fullness belongs to God. They know they are His ambassadors, that dominion is their calling, and that they were created to be in charge of the earth to rule in the place of Christ. When you believe this, supernatural encounters begin to take place in your life.

When you study lift and gravity, you will learn that lift does not do away with gravity; it employs it. However, you may say there is no such thing as lift; you may not believe it and can't even see it, yet when you see a plane flying, lift is what got it there.

An extremely important observation to make when we read the Word of God is that the manifestation of His Word requires nothing except His spoken word. Whatever God spoke, He brought out of the unseen realm into the seen realm.

The Scripture teaches that in speaking the Word of God, we become open for His Word to go down into the soil of our soul. We have all been carefully taught the truth concerning seed time and harvest time. It is true that every seed reproduces its own kind when you embrace the realm of the finished work and have an understanding that it is no longer you, but now it is Christ who lives in you.

As we consider the finished work in light of revelation versus reality we realize that many times we have knowledge of something with no experience. We say we understand the finished work, then still try to work things out on our own by dotting all the I's and crossing all the t's. If we have a revelation, we should have the emotions to back it up. If I have a revelation that I am accepted by the Lord but continuously feel rejected, then my emotions are telling me that my revelation is not lining up with my reality.

The understanding of God's Word only comes by being led by the Spirit. We want to get a formula that allows us to put check marks by our accomplishments, but God wants us to be flexible by working from a position of resting in wholeness and healing. In Him, says the Scripture, we live, and move, and have our being. We are already approved and loved.

You are not beggars and pleaders. All your needs have been judicially met in the unseen realm. It is with this understanding that you begin to release the Word of God, wealth, wisdom, knowledge, and grace over everything and everybody as the Holy Spirit leads. In this way, you are creating with God. You are pulling out of the then, and into the now. The words that you are speaking cause the manifestation of God's Word to be known. We must learn the Word of God not by the letter of the law, but by the Spirit. The law kills, but the Spirit brings life.

The following is a fun story that illustrates my point: A few years ago, my son-in-law bought a parrot whose name was Lola. He was telling me of his purchase and what a good deal he had received and that Lola was a very talkative bird.

He brought Lola home, but Lola would not say a word. She would sway back and forth, but she would never speak.

One day, Lola finally started talking, and this is what she would shriek out in an ear-splitting voice, "I'm soooooo sad. You make me

> *All your needs have been judicially met in the unseen realm. With this understanding begin to release the Word of God, wealth, wisdom, knowledge, and grace over everything and everybody as the Holy Spirit leads.*

wanna cry." You could hear her all over the neighborhood; I mean just screaming. My son-in-law finally decided, "We have to get rid of Lola. The neighbors a block away are hearing, "You make me wanna cry." After much time and effort, Lola eventually did learn to say my daughter's name, "Debra, Debra," but the way Lola said it would make anyone think someone was trying to kill Debra.

So my son-in-law tried to sell the bird, but nobody wanted it because poor Lola had been caged and had once been owned by a lady who was very depressed. The only thing the bird had ever heard was, "I'm so sad, and you make me wanna cry. You make me wanna cry." Lola learned to say the only thing she ever heard.

We are sort of like that. We say, "Repeat after me. Polly wants a cracker." The bird can say, "Polly wants a cracker," but doesn't know who Polly is, or what a cracker is. She has the letter of the law, but does not have the Spirit of truth inside her beak.

In like manner, there are things that we ask the Lord for, but when we get it, it is just not quite what we thought it was going to be or look like.

Lola somehow got delivered and began to sing a new song at the top of her lungs, "I love you, Debra." Within this story, however, we realize that Christians can be taught what to say; but, if there is no life or revelation behind it, it is a voice activation that produces nothing because there is no faith or understanding attached to it. We become like Lola in the Kingdom of God releasing all of these negative words that are summoning hell and the works of darkness. If Lola can be delivered from her foul speech, surely you and I can choose to agree with the Word of God.

Jesus has overcome hell, death and the grave and as a man thinks in His heart, so is he. It is for you and me and all the whosoevers who dare to believe and who set their affections on things above; who declare themselves to be a candidate for the restoration that God is doing in the earth today!

YES

The glory of God is Christ in you and me. There has to be something that swells up in your heart beyond the natural things of life. There has to be more in your mind and heart than the same old things that chew and erode at your faith.

I have learned that eternal life is not long life; rather it is the same quality of life that God is living. The Word of God teaches us that eye has not seen, nor ear heard what God has prepared for those who love Him. It is exceedingly abundantly above and beyond anything you can possibly think or imagine. He has revealed it by His Spirit. Choose to think from the perspective that you are called to be a nation of kings decreeing, declaring, proclaiming, and establishing God's truth.

We begin to see a picture of ourselves as we look in the Word of God. We can say we are the apple of God's eye. No weapons formed against us can prosper. Greater is He that is in us than He that is in the world. The devil is a defeated foe because Jesus took the keys to hell, death, and the grave, and now we are in charge.

To the normal, natural way of thinking, the ways of the Spirit are enmity, but God says that He is going to have a people who will believe that with God all things are possible. All things means "all" things! With God nothing is too hard! Regardless of the circumstances and the situations in your life, with God all things are possible. We have the tendency to get overwhelmed by the things that we see and hear, but the Scripture says eye has not seen and ear has not heard and neither has it entered into the heart of man the things which God has prepared. Who has He prepared these for? For those who love the Lord.

The Lord is calling you to exercise dominion. It does not have anything to do with gender, color, education, or status. You now have a new nature; you just look like a human. If you are going to pray God's Word, He sees it as already finished. The Spirit of God that is in you and makes intercession only prays the prayer that is already done. You are not capable and do not have the ability in your flesh and carnality to pray into the finished work.

Our carnal nature cannot perceive how to pray in accordance with the Word of God. The things of God become ours by the reason of use. Remember, God only prays from the revelation of what already is.

Jesus is seated at the right hand of the Father and lives forever to intercede for us. The only thing God watches over to perform is His word. From God's perspective, He has already met all of your needs. Learn how to activate that which already is and understand what the Word of God says; that faith comes by hearing, and hearing by the Word of God.

Information without Revelation
only Produces Imitation
that Leads to Stagnation.

You might think that the objective of God is to get you to heaven, but the reality is to get heaven through you into this earth realm. The way you release the Kingdom of God is with your words.

Chapter 7

Are you overwhelmed upon hearing the atrocities happening in various parts of the world; overwhelmed when you hear the word recession, or that the money is gone, this horror happened, and that tragedy took place?

The steps of the righteous are ordered by God. Everywhere you go you have been empowered to set the captives free. You are an ambassador sent from God to be a problem-solver.

The importance of the Word of God is that the Word spoken out of the believers is either going to activate hell or heaven. The Bible teaches that there is life and death in your mouth, so whatever you say, it will be. The same fire that cooks your food can burn your house down if it is not used correctly.

Remember, God's Word will never return void but will accomplish what it is sent forth to do. If we dwell and think in the unseen realm, that will place us where there are no limits and where it is boundless. As you stay in the unseen realm, you are anointed to bring heaven to this earth; so, as you go, say, "The kingdom of heaven has come, and it has come in me." Heal the sick, raise the dead, and cast out the devil.

The fact that you can quote the Scripture does not mean that it has become revelatory to you. Information without revelation only produces imitation that will lead to stagnation. Revelation is an unveiling of what is already here. The way you get revelation is to fellowship with the Holy Ghost and ask Him for revelation. You can have those "aha" moments where the revelation takes your breath away. You read a scripture verse and suddenly understand that what you just read has been there all your life yet you never saw it.

Because Jesus is the incarnate Word of God, whatever Jesus spoke was only that which He heard from His Father. Jesus understood His job assignment. We understand from God's Word that God is the operator of everything, Jesus is the administrator of the Kingdom of God, and the Holy Spirit manifests the will of God. It is no longer you who live, but Jesus who lives in you. As you go in life, you are to conduct the affairs of the Kingdom of God. Jesus said, "If you see Me, you've seen God." This is the empowerment to what already was by virtue of God's will. "As the Father sent Me, I am sending you. Now, go and act just like Me.' .... Wow!"

You might think that the objective of God is to get you to heaven, but the reality is to get heaven through you into this earth realm. The way you release the Kingdom of God is with your words. Your words can unveil what is already here.

One of the awesome purposes of Christ coming to this earth was to empower you and me to become what was already decreed from before the foundation of the earth. What is it that we are becoming? We are becoming the manifestation of the will of God, rather than succumbing to the deception of satan who thinks he has power. Satan has no power except what you give him. Jesus destroyed hell, death, and the grave. He has given us the keys to the Kingdom. As the Father sent Him, He sends us. Jesus emptied Himself of His divine nature and took the test in His full humanity. You are drawing hell to yourself with the words of your mouth and the meditation of your heart when your negative words are filled with unbelief.

One of the awesome purposes of Christ coming to this earth was to empower you and me to become what was already decreed from before the foundation of the earth.

I trust this begins to whet your appetite to see things from a different perspective. Jesus is encouraging each and every one of us as agents of His Word to release the dominion, power, and authority we have in this life. In the following chapters, we will learn about how to appropriate what is already here.

Notes

_____

_____

_____

_____

_____

_____

_____

_____

_____

_____

_____

_____

_____

_____

_____

_____

_____

_____

_____

_____

_____

_____

Don't Give Up!

When something goes amiss, God is lining you up for promotion. Many times, defeat and aggravation come right before great promotion.

Chapter 8

On a certain occasion, I followed a recipe to make a cheese soufflé. I do not know if any of you have ever made a cheese soufflé. It looked beautiful, but no one bothered to tell me that I could not bump the container while it is in the oven. If you bump the pan at the wrong time, the soufflé goes completely flat like a tasteless pancake. I did everything according to the word of the recipe. I followed it explicitly. There was just one thing that went wrong, and I imagine you can guess what that was! I closed the oven door abruptly. The results were not what I was hoping for. This experience did not stop me from trying again or believing that, because I had a negative experience, there was no such thing as an actual cheese soufflé. My second bump-less attempt turned out beyond my expectation. Keep trying!

When something goes amiss, God is lining you up for promotion. Many times, defeat and aggravation come right before great promotion.

This is not about sin. If you are being aligned for something really marvelous and wonderful, there are at least a couple of things you are going to experience which you would not necessarily recognize as coming from a divine place: things like discontentment and frustration. You begin to wonder if you really did hear God. All the negativity comes in; but God will simply tell you to take a deep breath and move on; to stand and not faint; to have faith that God is not only for you, He is with you. Correction is never rejection.

You Are Right on Time

Now we have received, not the spirit of the world, but the [Holy] Spirit who is from God, so that we may know and understand the [wonderful] things freely given to us by God – 1 Corinthians 2:12 (AMP).

Chapter 9

*K*ing Solomon said in Ecclesiastes 3:15, *Whatever is has already been, and what will be has been before; and God will call the past to account* (NIV). King Solomon already knew that from God's perspective, whatever is has already been, yet King Solomon activated his faith in God by asking God to give him the wisdom to rule God's people. King Solomon's request was granted as he apprehended what God had already prepared for him and was rightfully his. King Solomon was given wisdom, which is the ability to use knowledge skillfully. He activated, "Whatever is has already been, and what will be has been before."

If you settle for the familiar things in life, you will become a settler and your ability to see into the eternal provision of God can be limited. The familiar things will cause you to settle for less than what is rightfully yours. Take a step outside your familiar box. You cannot put new wine in an old wineskin.

Nor do they put new wine into old wineskins, or else the wineskins break, the wine is spilled, and the wineskins are ruined. But they put new wine into new wineskins, and both are preserved. – Matthew 9:17 (NKJV)

Everything that is seen, everything that is visible, has come from the unseen realm of God.

Every time you are tempted to think everything in life is getting darker, remember, God sits in the heavens and laughs, and holds His enemies in derision. He is not nervous about what is going on in the world, or anything else. God knows what is, and what has already been. He sees everything from His own perspective, which is the perfect finished work. It is up to you to strengthen yourself with the Word of God. Refuse to be depressed and resist the negative thoughts. When you encounter any of these temptations, immediately choose to be a part of a generation of overcomers that will rise up and refuse to accept the spirit of unbelief. God's Word says that your tradition makes His Word of no effect.

Making the word of God of none effect through your tradition, which ye have delivered: and many such like things do ye. – Mark 7:13 (KJV)

God waits for somebody to believe that He made it all, finished it, and then invited us to come and embrace everything from His perspective.

The activating Scripture in Romans 4:17 teaches, *. . . as it is written, "I have made you a father of many nations" in the presence of Him whom he believed—God, who gives life to the dead and <u>calls those things which do not exist as though they did</u>.*

You have to speak those things which be not, things that are not seen, as though they are. How do you do that? You do that by agreeing with and decreeing the Word of God. God's Word teaches that you are a legitimate heir with Christ on the earth. The fullness of God's promises belongs to me **now**; but, it is my responsibility and privilege to take dominion upon this earth. The Kingdom of God suffers violence, and the violent take it by force. The source of the force is the Holy Ghost. The source is always greater than the resource.

> *Agree with and decree the Word of God, which teaches that you are a legitimate heir with Christ on the earth. The fullness of God's promises belongs to you now.*

All of these tangible objects that we see have come into the natural realm from the spirit realm which actually resides within you, and it is called the Kingdom of God. The Kingdom of God calls us to walk as God's representatives in the earth. You must choose to let go of all the things that are preventing you from moving forward. Let God's Spirit arise in your midst with compassion, dominion, and power; where the lame leap, the blind see, the deaf hear, the dumb speak, demons are cast out, and the good news is declared. We are now open to receiving a transfer of wealth and inviting the wisdom of God to flow through us so that we will know how to administrate all that He has given. We can learn to talk, think, and act like God, our Heavenly Father.

As you believe and activate the process of taking command over your spoken words, you will then be open to a changed mind which is no longer ruled by the spirit of duality or double-mindedness. There must be a steadiness and a passion for what is going on within you for there dwells the Kingdom of God; or, you could find yourself full of information without any transformation and no life experience to endorse your words and actions.

We can no longer be satisfied with the traditional concept of getting just a little cabin in the corner of heaven and suggest to the Lord that we do not want to bother Him. God began His incredible work and has given us the Holy Spirit to help us understand the ways of God and be empowered to victoriously stand up to all circumstances and situations. First Corinthians 2:12 says, *Now we have received, not the spirit of the world, but the [Holy] Spirit who is from God, so that we may know and understand the [wonderful] things freely given to us by God (AMP).* This Scripture verse tells us that nothing we strive for can be fully acquired by human efforts alone.

As born-again believers, we have to understand that we carry the extraordinary nature and character of God. 2 Corinthians 5:17, *Therefore, if anyone is in Christ, he is a new creation; old things have passed away; behold, all things have become new. (NKJV)* We must continuously choose to stay teachable. Isn't it good to know that we are never too old or young to learn?

If you do not activate and place some pressure on what you say you believe and daily embrace some changes in your life, you are going to get to heaven, but it is doubtful you will take anybody with you.

We need to surround ourselves with those that are manifesting God's power and love, not just a lot of information.

Blessed are those who hunger and thirst for righteousness, for they shall be filled. (Matthew 5:6 NKJV).

Blessed are those who are hungry and thirsty for God. You are so blessed and empowered when you begin to experience a divine dissatisfaction with religion. You hunger and thirst for a real relationship with the Lord. You begin to know and understand that there is much more to this salvation message than what you are experiencing. Your heart hungers for true righteousness. Your heart begins to thirst for the powerful manifestation of Christ in your life.

I am so blessed to know that I am the righteous of God and my life is hidden in Christ. I am healed, delivered, prosperous, and the apple of His eye. All kinds of negative voices may be trying to tell you you're going down; just choose to get out of that sinking boat of your circumstances and walk on the water of the Word of God. Do you recall when Peter got out of the boat and walked on the water? Those who were with him possibly told him he was going to sink. Peter walked by faith, and those in the boat watched in unbelief. Have you ever tried to step out in faith and do what God told you to do but were surrounded by people who were trying to tell you that you do not meet the religious requirements or qualifications to serve until you do things a certain way? It is only the grace of God that will empower you to trust God.

If you are the righteousness of God, you have a new nature. Stop frustrating the grace of God by trying to earn your righteousness. This new nature will determine your actions and your will, and you will have a new heart to know and follow God.

I have these two dogs, Money and Debt Free, and I have never sent them to barking school. Their nature determines what they do. They bark at everything that moves. They have never meowed, and they do not chirp like a bird; but, if they did, I would make a lot of money. Your nature determines what you do. If I really believe I have the nature of God, I cannot do anything to earn that nature because the Scripture says I have received not the spirit of the world, but the Spirit which is of God. God has created and prepared everything for us. He did it before the foundation of the world; before sin ever came. He crucified Jesus, the antidote and the answer to all sin.

> *All kinds of negative voices may be trying to tell you you're going down; just choose to get out of that sinking boat of your circumstances and walk on the water of the Word of God.*

God is taking away the old nature to establish the new. The old way is revelation that was wonderful for another generation but there comes a transition time, such as now, when God invites you to lay down all the things that were so precious, wonderful, and fulfilling to you because they are not going to feed you anymore. There was a time when you loved all mashed up baby food on a spoon, but then you developed teeth and your pallet is different today! Although it is still food, you are not looking for pablum, but for strong meat that belongs to the mature who, by reason of use, have learned to exercise their senses to know that which is God and that which is not.

God is bringing us to a new diet; to the revelation of a fresh and wonderful new day. We are in transition as the new move of God is being birthed and labor pains are going on. During this time, the old nature has to move out to let the new nature move in!

Before the foundation of the world He knew when, where, who, and how to release what is best for us. This is the sovereignty of God; of knowing how to release out of this invisible unseen realm into the seen and manifested realm.

The following are three things you need to remember that can help you become a candidate to receive what God says is already yours:

1. **Trust God.** When you know you are truly hidden in Christ, then you are positioned to benefit from the manifestation of your destiny and breakthrough.

    When my husband and I were in the real estate business, we discovered a very important truth. You could change everything about a piece of property except its location. It is the location of the property that determines its value. What makes you valuable to the Kingdom of God is your location in Christ. You must be found in Christ. You are inside of Him, and He is inside of you. God knows when you are positioned in Him. That is when the benefit of the manifestation of your destiny occurs. The steps of the righteous are ordered by God. You are right on time.

2. Galatians 2:20 states *I am crucified with Christ: nevertheless, I live; yet not I, but Christ liveth in me: and the life which I now live in the flesh I live by the faith of the Son of*

God, who loved me, and gave himself for me (KJV). Once you know that it is no longer you, but now it is Christ in you; once you are positioned in Christ, then God knows He can trust you with anything and that you will be able to handle blessings that might come upon you. Let me give you an example. You have reckoned and esteemed the old nature dead, not sick. You cannot heal the old nature. You must starve the carnal nature to death by not feeding it words and thoughts that limit you. God is listening for His Word to come out of you.

3. God knows when we are spiritually mature enough to benefit others with our promised breakthrough.

What Eye Has not Seen, nor Ear Heard

We are entering into a time of coming into the fullness of God, and He is preparing a people to contain His fullness. Isn't there something in your heart that is saying, "I want everything that Jesus bought for me?"

Chapter 10

*I*n First Corinthians 2:9 it is written that, *Eye has not seen, nor ear heard, nor have entered into the heart of man the things which God has prepared for those who love him* (NKJV). "Eye has not seen, ear has not heard" – that is referring to your natural eyes and ears, as well as your natural mind and heart.

When your mind wonders how a thing is going to happen, remember that it is written that your eye has not seen, your ear has not heard, but in your spirit a light has turned on and illumination comes. There is an unveiling; a revealing of a spiritual truth that you had not previously known or recognized.

The Spirit of revelation cannot be learned or earned. It requires a consistent relationship with the Holy Spirit who is the teacher. As believers, we are dead to sin, and called and equipped to serve in the newness of the spirit.

Understand that you have been delivered from your old nature and that same spirit that raised Christ from the dead has quickened your mortal body and made you alive unto God. All power in heaven and earth has been given to you. Esteem yourself to new life every time you begin to create with the fruit of your lips.

That negative spirit that calls you sick, down, afflicted, mad, hurt, and wounded is nothing more than an evil spirit trying to rob you of your inheritance in Christ. God has already prepared everything you need to complete your body, soul, and spirit. He told us it was finished and decreed us healed, delivered, and prosperous.

As long as you continue to think with a carnal mind, the carnal mind cannot comprehend the things of God.

Because the carnal mind is enmity against God: for it is not subject to the law of God, neither indeed can be. – Romans 8:7 (KJV)

Everything is going to be a mystery to you. You need a renewed mind and then let the mind of Christ dwell in you richly. The Scripture says you have the mind of Christ whether you feel like you do or not. You can think that you do not prophesy or hear the voice of God. You cannot just keep magnifying your challenging circumstances and burying yourself with your negative words. Your deep desire to worship God is a way that deep calls unto deep.

The Holy Spirit empowers us to be witnesses. This was not intended to bring us to perfection, but to empower us to be witnesses of Jesus and His resurrection life. This empowering stirs us to hunger in our heart as deep calls out to deep and we realize that we are called to greater purposes. We discover that "something" has entered our eyes, "something" has entered our ears and heart and we realize a "Superman" lives inside of us that is knocking by day and night saying, "Let Me out. Let Me out." We know that something is about to take place; an eruption beyond "business as usual" and beyond the "same ole, same ole;" beyond just waiting to someday fly away to Jesus.

We are entering into a time of coming into the fullness of God, and He is preparing a people to contain His fullness. Isn't there something in your heart that is saying, "I want everything that Jesus bought for me?" For instance, consider if someone bought you an expensive Mercedes Benz and didn't give you the key. As wonderful as the Mercedes Benz is, you need the key to make it run.

In the same way, Jesus has come that we may have life; and life more exceedingly and abundantly. You may have the promise, but you need the key to turn it on. You need your spiritual eyes and spiritual ears opened. You need healing in your body, and your home and finances restored. You need your joy, peace, and the reality of all that God says is yours! The devil says, "Now, you just sit down. This isn't for you. You're going to have to die and then you'll get it all in heaven." Understand that Jesus died, and heaven came down to you! The

You may have the promise, but you need the key to turn it on. You need your spiritual eyes and spiritual ears opened. You need healing in your body, and your home and finances restored. You need your joy, peace, and the reality of all that God says is yours!

Kingdom of God is within you. You can go through this life, die, and go to heaven and not go to hell, but to what degree do you believe the Kingdom of God is within you? There is a torrent of the knowing of the purposes of the love of God. There is a generation, a remnant who will behold the King in His Glory.

Moses stood on Mount Nebo and viewed the promised land. One of the main things that gave Moses a problem was that the people provoked him. The first time God spoke to Moses, He told him to strike the rock so that water would come. The second time God spoke to Moses, He told him to speak to the rock and the water would come. The people, however, had so aggravated, frustrated, and provoked Moses that he went back and embraced the thing that worked the first time. God reminded Moses that he struck it the first time, and now Moses was being instructed to just speak. Whatsoever things you say in My name, it shall be done. You do not have to fight, and you do not have to strike, you simply need to speak; but, Moses employed the old way. In return, Moses never got to stand on the promised land. He could only look at it from a distance.

You say, "Lord, I want You to show Yourself and be expressed in my life. I want your power, purity, and love to show through me." God then says, "Lay down your life then, that I may come up." The King of Glory is knocking at the door of your heart saying, "Let Me out!" You ask, "Lord, how? How do I let the King of Glory out?" Let the words of your mouth and the meditation of your heart be acceptable to God. Put a guard over your eyes, over your ears, and over your mouth so that you will only say the things you hear God say.

There are some things that are required of us. One of those requirements is that we need to pay attention to God's Word. We have been equipped with everything we will ever need, and are lacking nothing.

Notes

God Sees the End at the Beginning

If God framed, completely placed in order, all His worlds with His Word, then you and I are going to have to frame our worlds with the Word of God. Our decisions have to be made by the Word of God.

Chapter 11

I want to review the premise that we began with originally. We are studying about seeing the unseen realms of God. We know that everything we see came out of an unseen realm, and that God has called us as believers to have dominion and power in this earth.

It was over before it began. Jesus was crucified in the counsels of glory before the foundation of the earth; before anything happened. God has already told us that any problem there is ever going to be, He already solved before we do anything. He framed the worlds with His Word.

God sees the end at the beginning. He understands that everything necessary for us to make a 100% on our test in life has already been supplied. I think that is an amazing thing that ought to excite you and make you laugh hysterically. As a child, I would stand on my Daddy's toes and he would dance with me. He made me feel very successful and protected. I am learning to dance on Father God's toes. He makes me look really good.

> *Before I formed you in the womb I knew you [and approved of you as My chosen instrument], And before you were born I consecrated you [to Myself as My own];I have appointed you as a prophet to the nations. – Jeremiah 1:5 (AMP)*

If we have always been, even before we knew our mother's womb, and always will be, then we begin to understand that God is not limited. He created us in such a way that He downloaded into our being things in our spirit that our soul and body have not yet apprehended. I refer to this as God's DNA impartation; Divine Nature Attitude.

There are times when we are seeking the presence of the Lord and praying the Word of God that revelatory things begin to happen. You might say something as simple as; "Father, I just thank You, praise You, and bless You." Suddenly, you catch the wind of the Spirit and you get into a flow, your spirit jumps up, and you begin to understand things that you did not understand before.

When you begin to study and have a revelation of the finished work, you will understand that Jesus is the Son of God, and that He calls you blessed because you are a people who know by revelation that flesh and blood did not reveal this to you but your Father who is in Heaven. Those things which have been unveiled, revealed, and quickened to you are like bullets in your spiritual arsenal. That is when you launch out and say, "It is written, it is written, it is written. It is not just something that has not been quickened to me. All of the Word is good, but there are certain truths that have been established in me when I agree with His Word that it is established."

Through faith we understand that the worlds were framed, and that you and I were made in the image and likeness of God. We are like cells in His body; little orbits of creation, if you will.

If God framed, completely placed in order, all His worlds with His Word, then you and I are going to have to frame our worlds with the Word of God. Our decisions have to be made by the Word of God.

Everything that is manifested from the unseen realm comes by the activating of the Word of God which causes things to be seen. This unseen realm is not over some great mystical wall; it is in you and is called the hope of glory. What is glory? Glory is the manifestation of Jesus plainly seen. Who is Jesus? He is the Word of God made flesh. Who are you? You are heirs of God and joint-heirs with Christ. We are Christ's ambassadors in this world.

You are not going to see the things you desire if you are not activating the Word of God by speaking it. The spoken word is spoken only that we might become what we already are.

We are learning in the sweet presence of God to see the realm of the invisible and begin to say, "Father, I just thank You. I am going to create with You by agreeing with Your Word. I am not going to frustrate Your grace. You, Lord, are my shepherd. I want to see the goodness of the Lord in the land of the living, to see myself walking debt free in prosperity, and see health and wholeness. I want to hear a new testimony of something incredible happening when I pray for arms and legs to grow where they weren't formed. I want to see an unveiling of the Christ that is in me, so I repent of being one that would stand back and allow circumstances to dictate to me what the covenant of God has for me."

> *My eye has not seen, my ear has not heard, and neither has it entered my heart what God has prepared for the heart of man; but, in my spirit I have perceived the King in His beauty filling all the earth with His glory.*

My eye has not seen, my ear has not heard, and neither has it entered my heart what God has prepared for the heart of man; but, in my spirit I have perceived the King in His beauty filling all the earth with His glory. I will perceive walking above death, doom, destruction, weakness and limitation. This is not that I would be exalted, but that all He purchased for me would be realized on planet earth. I believe that I will live to see the goodness of the Lord in the land of the living. This is beyond the status quo. This needs to give you some hope, and some fire! We are coming out of a tunnel and making a turn. There is a new day dawning, and we desire to be a part of it!

We are seeing the Word of God coming forth out of the believers of God. His people are learning to pray the Word of God. As a result, powers in heaven are being shaken. He is going to shake heaven and earth and, everything that is not of Him and fashioned as a life support system is going to fall! Is your life being shaken? Is there anything in your life that is not being shaken? You may say, "God, I believe in healing," and yet your body is under attack. You may say, "Lord, I believe in prosperity," and you can't even pay a bill. You may say, "Lord, I believe that all my children are disciples taught of the Lord," and yet they are all going crazy. You may say, "Lord, I believe that my household is in order," and then your spouse walks out. There is no answer except that you know Calvary is a finished work. The facts say one thing, but the Word of God is clear and says hold fast to the precious promises, for eye has not seen, and ear has not heard; neither has it entered into the hearts of man what God has for those who love Him. God says, "See Me, hear Me, and make your heart fixed on Me!"

As you desire to come closer and closer to God you begin to understand that your life has already been planned out. He knows exactly every hair on your head; knows everything about you.

> In whom also we have obtained an inheritance, being predestinated according to the purpose of him who worketh all things after the counsel of his own will. – Ephesians 1:11 (KJV)

For God's pleasure, we were created. What an incredible thing. It is not about what we do. We were made to make God happy, and to believe Him.

You have now come to the point where you understand the steps you need to take in:

Release God's Word to every Life Situation and Watch it Work!
Yes, Release the Power of God's Word over Your Life and Family!

In the following pages, I invite you to activate all you have learned by incorporating your knowledge into your every life situation and experience.

And then, I'll meet you on the other side of " Activation" as we close out our time together in prayer.

Activation

Chapter 12

What is your understanding of the "Kingdom" of God?

_____

_____

_____

_____

_____

Describe a time when you got a glimpse of the demonstrations and manifestations of the power of God.

_____

_____

_____

_____

_____

_____

What desires do you have in the "someday" realm that you would like to move into the "now" realm?

_____

_____

_____

_____

_____

_____

Think back, and describe a time when your challenge became a once-in-a-lifetime opportunity.

_____

_____

_____

_____

_____

_____

Has there ever been a time when you heard God's voice speak to your spirit? What was the outcome?

_____

_____

_____

_____

_____

_____

Describe a time when something happened in your life
where there was no natural explanation.

_____

_____

_____

_____

_____

_____

List some things that you are "daring" to believe.

_____

_____

_____

_____

_____

_____

_____

Describe a time in your life when you were presented with
an "opportunity" that looked like something other than an
"opportunity."

_____

_____

_____

_____

Make a list of those who support your vision and purpose, and then describe the way in which these people support what you are carrying.

_____

_____

_____

_____

_____

Have you ever had an occasion when something that was said caused something inside of you to leap for joy because you knew it was specifically for you? Describe the events surrounding this occasion.

_____

_____

_____

_____

_____

Given what you have read, what is your understanding of "every seed reproduces its own kind?"

_____

_____

_____

_____

_____

Describe a time when you purchased, achieved, or attained something and, once you brought it home and attempted to apply it to your life, it did not look or act like you thought it would.

_____

_____

_____

_____

_____

Make a list of areas in your life that you now see as being in need of a "commanding" voice activation.

_____

_____

_____

_____

_____

Have you ever had an occasion in your life when God's law superseded natural law? If you answered yes, please describe the event.

_____

_____

_____

_____

_____

In what ways do you believe your steps have been ordered by God?

_____

_____

_____

_____

_____

_____

How have you framed your world? Paint a written verbal picture of your framed world.

_____

_____

_____

_____

_____

_____

Have you ever had an occasion when you saw the visible manifestation of your own spoken words? Please describe.

_____

_____

_____

_____

_____

_____

ACTIVATION

Describe your understanding of "set times and seasons."

_____

_____

_____

_____

_____

Describe a situation that looked very bleak but turned
out to be the beginning of a new chapter in your life.

_____

_____

_____

_____

_____

List some ways your perspective has changed from the
way you saw things before you started reading this book.

_____

_____

_____

_____

_____

_____

In what ways do you see yourself differently now than you did at the beginning of this book?

_____

_____

_____

_____

_____

_____

How do you activate the Word of God?

_____

_____

_____

_____

_____

_____

Describe the finished work.

_____

_____

_____

_____

_____

_____

We Are Called to Walk in Dominion.

Closing Prayer

Father, I thank You for our time together. Thank You that Your Word has the power to activate, and that it brings forth the wonderful things that are already done. We shall ask what we will and it shall be done. The Word of God goes forth, and anything that would cause doubt, fear, or frustration in our lives, we simply say we are done with it. Lord, thank You that we are rising to fresh plateaus of understanding and are filled with the Word that is spoken.

Thank You, Lord, that we have learned we are people walking in the dimension of undiscovered resources. We understand that as deep calls unto deep, by faith we are healed, delivered, and prosperous. Lord, thank You that we are a new creation. Father, I thank You that You know when we are positioned to benefit from the manifestation of our breakthrough, and that You know when we are spiritually mature enough to benefit others. I thank You that the Spirit of revelation is upon each and every one of us and that You are quickening and making it alive to those that You have called us to understand. Thank You that we are positioned to speak as the oracles of God, and create with the fruit of our lips.

Father, I thank You that, from Your perspective, everything is finished. Your works have been completed, prepared, and are waiting for all who would just believe from the foundation of the world. What is present has already been. Lord, we thank You that, through faith, we understand spiritual things that are not understandable in the natural. Everything that we see comes from Your unseen invisible creative will. Teach us to speak Your Word and how to create with You as heirs of God and joint heirs with Christ.

Lord, thank You for calling us to walk in dominion, and showing us what our position in Christ is. Amen!

About Dr. Clarice Fluitt

Dr. Clarice Fluitt is an internationally recognized Christian leader, author, and popular television personality. For more than four decades, she has had a distinguished world-wide reputation as a Christian mentor. Her success is based on her ability to assist ministries, organizations, and individuals achieve real results. Her experiences as a mentor, enterprising businesswoman, and strategic consultant allow her to share her proven strategies for building the Kingdom, inspiring individuals, and generating sustainable growth.

Dr. Fluitt is a time-proven prophetess with laser like accuracy. Reports of amazing miracles and healings with positive life changing evidence continually follow her ministry. Dr. Clarice's life is a remarkable chronicle of hilarious real-life stories, tragic trials, tests, and moving visitations of the Lord. Unpretentious and friendly, she is a highly-esteemed minister and conference speaker.

Drawing from her background in marketplace and Christian ministry, national and international church and mentoring school training and development, leadership expertise, and world-wide speaking engagements, Dr. Fluitt touches lives through her wisdom, wit, and extraordinary insight, providing avenues of transformational change to individuals from every walk of life.

More Resources by Dr. Clarice Fluitt

Books

- **Ridiculous Miracles**
- **The Law of Honor**
- **Inspirational Insights**
- **Thoughts That Make You Think**
- **Developing Your Limitless Potential**
- **Living the Unhindered Life**
- **... and introducing ...**

Think Like a Champion and Win!

This is the ultimate in restoring your focus, your resolve, and your commitment to living beyond limiting beliefs. After all, champions live differently than ordinary people. Say to yourself, "There's more to me than what you see!"

Tell yourself that you are a winner and you will see change manifest before your very eyes. Learn how to create lasting changes and complete what you start through the process of discovery and discipline. This book will assist you in clarifying the results you desire, deciding on new actions to take, and recognizing the potential within you.

New Release!

Think Like a Champion and Win goes beyond the boundaries of a book and into the land of solution. Failure is just an illusion.

Experience Major Breakthrough and Progressive Successes as you Think Like a Champion and Win!

Available at www.claricefluitt.com/shop

Notes

Notes

Notes

Notes

Notes

Notes

Notes

Notes

Notes

Notes

Notes

Notes

Champions live differently than ordinary people!

To Book Dr. Clarice for Speaking:

www.claricefluitt.org

Clarice Fluitt Ministries
P.O. Box 7888
Monroe, LA 71211-7888

For information on Real Results Real Solutions
Coaching & Mentoring Packages:

www.claricefluitt.com

Clarice Fluitt Enterprises, LLC
P.O. Box 15111
Monroe, LA 71207

Special Invitation

Are you ready for real results?

Dr. Clarice invites you to a time of impartation and personal mentoring.

A master coach and personal advisor with keen prophetic insight and great wisdom, Dr. Clarice invites you to join her in a special mentoring group. For the unbelievable price of $97.00 your registration will guarantee for you:

- Personal Assessment Questionnaire
- TWO Live 90 Minute Group Interactive Calls
- An MP3 Recording of each Live Session
- Dr. Clarice's personal attention to the issues that matter most to you!

For dates, details, and to register please visit:
www.claricefluitt.com/impartation-and-mentoring/

Only $97!
Limited Time Offer, Register Today!